The Berenstain Bears®
Storybook
Bible

Jan & Mike Berenstain

ZONDERVAN.com/
AUTHORTRACKER
follow your favorite authors

Living
Lights™

ZONDERkidz

ZONDERKIDZ

The Berenstain Bears® Storybook Bible
Copyright © 2013 by Berenstain Publishing, Inc.
Illustrations © 2013 by Berenstain Publishing, Inc.

Requests for information should be addressed to:
Zonderkidz, 5300 Patterson Ave. SE, Grand Rapids, Michigan 49530

ISBN 978-0-310-72721-7

Editor: Mary Hassinger
Cover and interior design: Cindy Davis

Printed in the United States

13 14 15 16 17 /DCI/ 10 9 8 7 6 5 4 3 2 1

It was time for Papa Bear to read Brother,
Sister, and Honey a bedtime story. But the cubs
couldn't agree on a story. Brother wanted an
exciting story about Space Grizzlies. Sister wanted
a nice story about princesses. Honey wanted a
happy story about bunnies or chipmunks.

"Let's read a Bible story," said Papa. "The Bible has all kinds of stories—exciting ones, nice ones, happy ones, even serious ones."

The cubs liked Bible stories. They were all about sword fights and floods and wild animals—all sorts of interesting things.

"Okay," Brother and Sister agreed. And even Honey clapped.

So Papa got out the storybook Bible and began to read. The cubs had fun imagining that all the characters in the stories were bears, just like them!

The Old Testament
In the Beginning: Genesis 1

In the beginning
God made the heaven and the earth.
First, all was dark.

But God said, "Let there be light."
And there was light.
God called the light "day."
He called the darkness "night."
That was the first day.
And it was very good!

God said, "Let the heavens appear."
The heavens stretched over great waters.

God called the heavens "sky." That was
the second day. And it was very good!

God made dry land appear. God called the water "sea" and he called the land "earth." God covered the earth with plants and trees. That was the third day. And it was very good!

God made the sun and
the moon, the planets
and the stars. He placed
them in the heavens.
That was the fourth day.
And it was very good!

God made all the creatures that live in the sea and fly in the air. He made the great whales and the fish and the birds. That was the fifth day. And it was very good!

17

God made all the animals that live on the earth. He made deer and giraffes, hippos and lions, bugs and slugs, turtles and frogs. Then he made a man and a woman. They were called Adam and Eve. God saw that it was all good. That was the sixth day.

On the seventh day,
God rested. God blessed
the seventh day because it
was his special day of rest.

21

Adam and Eve: Genesis 2

When God made the earth, he planted a garden in the east, in Eden, and placed Adam there. In the middle of the garden there was a beautiful fruit tree. God told Adam that he could eat anything in the garden except the fruit of that tree.

When Adam first got to the garden, he gave names to all the animals.

But Adam became lonely.
So God created Eve.

Together, Adam and Eve cared for the garden and lived in peace with all the animals.

The snake was the slyest of all animals in the garden. He came to Eve one day and said, "The fruit of the tree in the middle of the garden looks very sweet. Why don't you taste it?"

But Eve said, "God said we should not eat it."

And the snake said, "Try it, anyway!"

So Eve ate the fruit and shared some with Adam too.

After they ate the fruit, Adam and Eve knew they had
done something wrong. They were frightened, and hid
themselves in the garden. But God knew what Adam and
Eve had done. He was sad that they had not obeyed him
and he was angry with that sneaky snake!

God said to the snake, "Because you have done this, you must crawl on your belly from now on!"

The snake crawled away and snakes have been crawling ever since.

To Adam and Eve, God said, "Since you have not followed the rules in my garden, you must go out and grow your own food."

Adam and Eve had to leave the garden. God placed angels and a flaming sword to guard the entrance. Adam and Eve could not go back.

They went out into the world and began to
farm the land. And they had many children.

Noah's Ark: Genesis 6

After many years, God saw that most of the people on the earth were doing evil things.

God decided that he should destroy all life on earth and start over.

35

But there was one man, Noah,
who was a good man.

God wanted to save him, so he warned Noah that a great flood was coming. He told Noah to build a giant boat, called an ark. He was to take his family and two of every kind of creature, male and female, into the ark with him.

Noah started to build the ark. His whole family helped him. They worked hard! It took a very long time to build the ark. But they knew they had to finish it before the great flood. Other people watched Noah's family at work. The people were puzzled. They could not figure out why Noah was building such a huge boat.

Finally, the ark was finished. Noah and his family began to gather all the food they would need during the flood. It was a very big job. They needed food for themselves and food for all the animals that would be in the ark with them.

When everything was ready, God sent all the animals, two by two, to the ark. Noah checked the different kinds off on a long list. It took many days for all the animals to march on board.

Noah's family led the animals to stalls and pens inside the ark and birds perched up on the beams. When all the creatures were safe on board, God shut up the doors and windows of the ark.

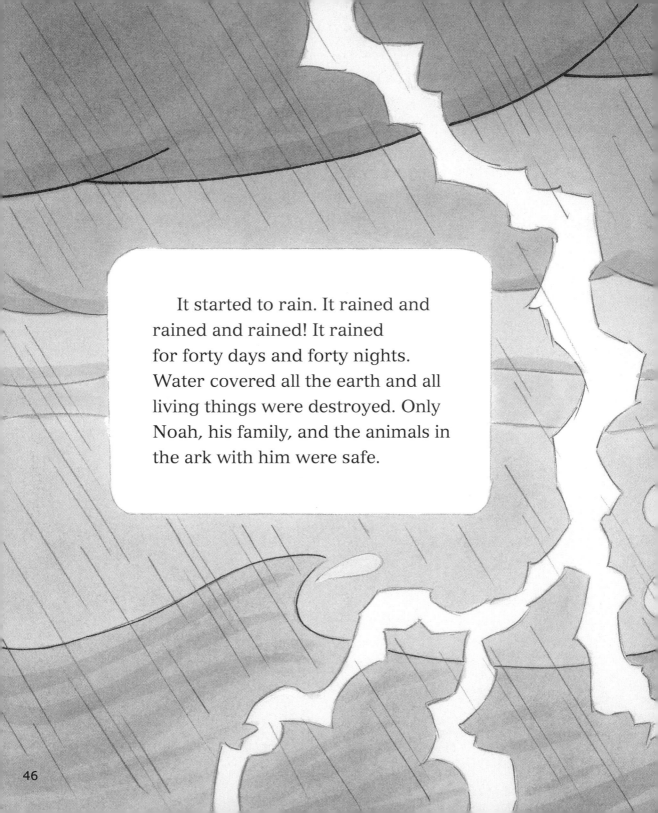

It started to rain. It rained and
rained and rained! It rained
for forty days and forty nights.
Water covered all the earth and all
living things were destroyed. Only
Noah, his family, and the animals in
the ark with him were safe.

When the rain finally stopped,
the water began to go down. The ark
came to rest on a mountaintop. But
there was still water over all the earth.

Noah sent out a raven to see if there was dry land anywhere. The raven did not come back.

Then, Noah sent out a dove. The dove came back with an olive leaf in its beak, so Noah knew it was safe to go out.

All the animals soon left the ark. Happily, they galloped and crawled and flew out onto the dry land. Noah gave thanks to God that they were safe. Then Noah saw a rainbow in the clouds. It was a sign from God that he would not bring so great a flood on the earth, again.

The Tall Tower: Genesis 11

After the flood, everyone in the world spoke
the same language. The people decided to
show their power by building a great tower
that would reach up to heaven. Thousands of
people gathered to help build the tower.

First, the people made bricks to build the tower.
Then they set to work. They worked very hard.
The tower began to rise. It rose higher and higher
toward heaven.

57

But God did not want the people to build a tower up to heaven. He knew it was not good for them to have such power. They would think they had more power than even God and they would become wicked.

So, God made all the people speak different languages. Suddenly, the people found they could not understand each other. They grew angry and got in fights about how to do their work.

Everyone gave up working on the tower. They left it unfinished and went off in different directions to live all over the world. That is how people began to speak different languages.

Joseph and his Brothers: Genesis 37

Jacob was a man chosen by God to be the father of a nation called Israel. His twelve sons would be the leaders of the twelve tribes of Israel.

Jacob's favorite son was named Joseph. One day,
Jacob gave Joseph a special coat made of many colors.
And that made his brothers jealous.

Joseph went looking for his brothers.
When they saw him coming in his special
coat, the brothers felt so jealous that they
stole his coat and threw him down in a pit.
They left him there to die.

Some traders who were on their way to Egypt soon came by. The brothers had a new plan. They would sell Joseph to these traders! They pulled Joseph out of the pit and sold him.

Then Joseph was taken to Egypt. There, the traders sold him as a slave in the palace of Pharaoh, the king.

One of Joseph's brothers, named Reuben, felt guilty about what they had done and went back for Joseph. But he was gone.

So, Reuben asked his brothers to tear Joseph's coat and put blood on it. They told their father Jacob that Joseph had been killed by a wild animal. Jacob was very sad and wept for his lost son.

In Egypt, Joseph worked hard. He was given a
job by an important man in Pharaoh's palace. Before
long, Joseph heard that Pharaoh had a dream that
worried him.

Pharaoh wanted to know what his dream meant, and Joseph was good at explaining dreams. So, he explained Pharaoh's dream to him. Pharaoh was pleased and put Joseph in charge of his palace.

Many years later, Joseph's brothers had to travel to Egypt to buy food because there was not enough food in their land. They came to the palace and asked Joseph to sell them food. They did not recognize Joseph. But he recognized them! At first, he was angry with them and had his brothers put in prison.

Later, Joseph changed his mind. He felt sorry for his brothers and let them out of prison. Finally, Joseph told them who he was. They all wept and hugged each other.

Then, they brought their father down to Egypt to join them. Jacob was very happy to find his long, lost son. Jacob's people, the Israelites, all moved to Egypt with him.

The Story of Moses: Exodus 1

A new Pharaoh ruled in Egypt. He did not like the Israelites. He made them work very hard. Pharaoh thought there were too many Israelites and decided to get rid of all their baby boys.

One Israelite woman tried to save her baby boy. She put him in a basket and left him by the river's edge.

The daughter of the Pharaoh came down to the river and found the basket with the little baby crying inside. She felt sorry for him and decided to raise him as her own son. He grew up to be a prince of Egypt, and was called Moses.

When Moses grew up, he learned he was an Israelite. He became angry about how badly his people were treated by Pharaoh.

He ran away from Egypt and lived
in the desert herding sheep.

One day, while watching his flock on a mountain, Moses saw a burning bush. It was on fire but its leaves did not burn up. A voice came from the bush. It was the voice of God.

God told Moses that he wanted him to go back to Egypt and tell Pharaoh to let all the Israelites go free. Moses was to lead God's people out of Egypt. Moses did not think he could do it alone. God told Moses he would be helped by his brother, Aaron. So Moses obeyed God.

When Moses went back to Egypt, he went with his brother, Aaron, to Pharaoh.

"The Lord says, 'Let my people go!'" they told Pharaoh.

But Pharaoh would not let the Israelites go. So God punished Pharaoh and all of Egypt.

First, God turned the water of the river Nile
into blood. All the fish in the river died and no one
could drink the water.

But Pharaoh still refused to let the people go.

God punished Pharaoh again and again. God sent frogs, insects, sickness, hail, locusts, and darkness over the land of Egypt.

But Pharaoh still would
not let the people go.

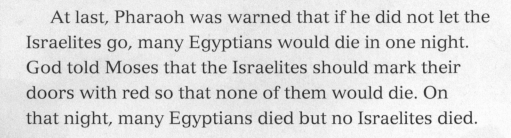

At last, Pharaoh was warned that if he did not let the Israelites go, many Egyptians would die in one night. God told Moses that the Israelites should mark their doors with red so that none of them would die. On that night, many Egyptians died but no Israelites died.

Finally, Pharaoh agreed to let God's people go.

The Israelites gathered all their belongings together, all their food and their animals. And Moses led them out of Egypt, across the desert to a new land.

The Ten Commandments: Exodus 14

After the Israelites left Egypt, Pharaoh grew angry
again. He changed his mind about letting them go.
So, he took his army and went after them.

Moses led God's people to the shores of a wide sea called the Red Sea. He did not know how to get across. Then, they all saw the army of the Pharaoh coming up behind.

Moses lifted up his staff and asked God to help them. God parted the waters of the Red Sea and the people were able to walk across.

Once the people were across, Pharaoh and his men tried to follow them. But the waters came crashing down on the army and they were destroyed.

Moses and the people gave thanks to God for saving them.

While Moses was leading the Israelites to their new land, they grew hungry and thirsty. Moses asked God for help. Pieces of bread, called manna, fell from the sky to feed the people.

Moses struck a rock with his staff and a spring of fresh water gushed out. The people were saved.

God led the Israelites to a mountain in the wilderness. There, God called Moses to the top of the mountain and said, "I am the Lord your God who brought you out of Egypt."

Then God gave Moses two stone tablets with ten rules written on them.

Samson: Judges 16

The strongest man in the land of Israel was Samson. He was so strong he could carry the gates of a town away on his back.

He could kill an attacking lion with his bare hands. In battle, Samson could defeat whole armies with only an old bone for a weapon.

Samson was in love with a beautiful woman named Delilah. The enemies of Israel told Delilah that they would pay her if she found out what made Samson so strong.

So, Delilah asked Samson to tell her his secret. At first
Samson would not tell her. But she begged him and finally
he told her that his strength was in his long hair. If his
hair were cut off, Samson would be weak.

One night, while Samson was sleeping, Delilah had someone cut off his hair. She called enemy soldiers to take him prisoner. Samson woke up and tried to fight but now he was weak. The soldiers tied him up and blinded him.

115

They took Samson to the temple of his enemies and tied him between two pillars. The temple was filled with people who made fun of him. Samson prayed to God, asking God to give him his strength once more. Samson's strength came back.

Samson pushed against the pillars
and the whole temple came crashing
down, destroying Samson along with
his enemies.

David and Goliath: 1 Samuel 17

David was a young shepherd in Israel. It was his job to watch over his father's flock of sheep. David knew that God was with him, so he was not afraid of wolves or lions.

He used his sling to throw stones at these beasts to drive them away.

David's older brothers went away to join King Saul who was fighting the enemies of Israel. In the enemy's army there was a warrior named Goliath. Goliath towered over all other warriors. No one was brave enough to fight him.

Goliath went out between the two armies.

"Why don't you come fight me?" he called. "Pick one of your warriors to come out and fight me. Whoever wins will win the war."

But no one in the army of Israel was brave enough to fight the giant, Goliath.

One day, David's father sent him to take food to his brothers in the army. When David got there, he heard Goliath's challenge. David was not afraid. He knew that God was watching over him. He told his brothers that he would go out and fight Goliath.

"But you are just a boy!" laughed his brothers.

David still said he would fight Goliath.

King Saul heard about what David was saying and sent for him. He told David that he was too young to fight Goliath. But David explained that he used his sling and stones to drive off lions and wolves to protect his flock of sheep. He said he could do the same with Goliath.

So King Saul gave David a man's armor, a big helmet, and a huge sword. But they were too big for David. He couldn't even walk in them.

David took off the armor, helmet, and sword.
He gathered some stones and, with his sling,
went out to meet Goliath.

When Goliath saw David, he laughed because David was only a boy.

"Am I a dog that they send children to fight me?" he called.

He raised his great spear to throw it at David.

But David quickly put a stone in his sling and swung it around and around his head. He let it fly, and the stone struck Goliath right in the middle of his forehead.

BONK!

Goliath fell to the ground with a crash that shook the earth. Little David had struck down the giant warrior. With God's help, David saved Israel.

David the Singer: 1 Samuel 21–23; Psalm 23

Before David fought Goliath, he helped King Saul in another way. It happened that King Saul could not sleep at night. Every night, he lay awake, tossing and turning.

It also happened that David was a good singer and harp player. Everyone who heard him said his music was among the best in all Israel.

King Saul heard about what a good singer David was too. He thought that listening to music might help him sleep. So King Saul sent for David.

Every evening, David sat by King Saul's bed and played soft music. The music made King Saul's eyes slowly close and he fell asleep. King Saul was very pleased with David and kept him with him in the palace.

Later in his life, David was chosen to be the king of all Israel. He was a good king and a great leader of his people in battle.

But he also kept on singing and playing the harp. He wrote and sang many songs, called psalms, in praise of God.

One of the most famous songs of David
is the Twenty-Third Psalm:

The Lord is my shepherd, I lack nothing.
He makes me lie down in green pastures,
he leads me beside quiet waters,
he refreshes my soul.

He guides me along the right paths
for his name's sake.
Even though I walk
through the darkest valley,
I will fear no evil,
for you are with me;
your rod and your staff,
they comfort me.

You prepare a table before me
in the presence of my enemies.
You anoint my head with oil;
My cup overflows.
Surely your goodness and love will
follow me all the days of my life,
and I will dwell in the house
of the Lord forever.

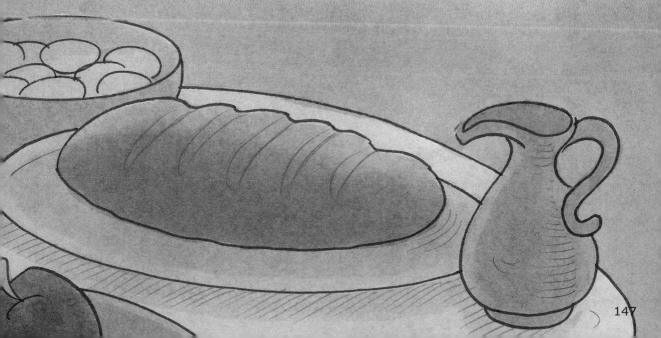

Esther the Queen: Esther 1-10

Long after the days of David, many Israelites were carried off to the kingdom of Persia, to be slaves for the people there.

The queen of Persia was a beautiful woman named Vashti. The king was very proud of her great beauty.

The king asked Vashti to come to a feast in the palace and sit beside him. But Vashti did not want to sit with all the people and she refused. This made the king angry. He decided he would have a new queen. He sent word out into his kingdom to send beautiful young women to the palace. He would choose his new queen from among them.

Among the people of Israel was a man named Mordecai. He was a loyal servant of the king. He had an adopted daughter named Esther. Esther was the most beautiful young woman in all the land.

Mordecai sent her to the king's palace to try to be chosen as his new queen. When the king saw Esther, he at once fell in love with her and made her his new queen.

The king had an important helper named Haman. Haman was very rich and powerful. But Haman did not like Mordecai. He felt that Mordecai did not show him enough respect. So Haman decided to get rid of Mordecai and all of Mordecai's people.

But Queen Esther found out about Haman's plan.
She went to the king and told him that Mordecai had
been a good servant of the king. Then, she invited
Haman to eat with her and with the king.

While they ate, Esther told the king that someone was planning to kill his servant Mordecai and all the Israelite people. The king grew angry and asked who it was who dared to do this.

Queen Esther told the king it was Haman who was plotting to do this. At once, the king had Haman arrested and put to death. Queen Esther had saved her people!

Daniel in the Lions' Den: Daniel 6

At one time, some of the Israelites were taken to the land of Babylon to be servants. The king of the land made one of the Israelites, Daniel, his chief servant. But the king's other servants were jealous of Daniel and his power. They got the king to make a new law saying that the people of Israel could not pray to God.

But Daniel went on praying to
God and the king found out.

The king liked Daniel and did not want to hurt him. But he did not want to go against his own law either. So, he ordered that Daniel be put to death by throwing him into a den of savage lions. Daniel was thrown in the lions' den and the den was closed up.

The next day, the king came to open the den. When the king and his servants looked inside, they saw Daniel petting the lions! One of the lions was licking Daniel's hand. Everyone was amazed to find that Daniel was unhurt.

The king was happy his servant, Daniel, was safe. He understood that God had protected Daniel. So the king made a law saying that all in the land should respect Daniel's God, and that Daniel and his people should worship him in peace.

Jonah and the Great Fish: Jonah 1

Jonah was a prophet of God. God told him to go to the city of Nineveh and teach the people to stop doing wicked things. But Jonah did not want to go. Instead, he ran away. He got on a ship to cross the sea. As Jonah sailed away on the ship, a great storm came. The sailors were afraid the ship would sink.

Jonah told the sailors that God was angry with him. He said that to save their ship, they should throw him overboard. And that is what the frightened sailors did.

Jonah sank down under the waves and was swallowed by a great fish.

Inside the belly of the fish, Jonah prayed to God.

"Oh Lord, all your waves are passed over me. Yet I will look toward your holy temple. Salvation is of the Lord."

God heard Jonah's prayer and made the fish spit Jonah out on dry land. Then God told Jonah, again, to go and preach in Nineveh. This time, Jonah obeyed.

The New Testament
The Birth of Jesus: Luke 1

A young woman named Mary lived in the city of Nazareth. An angel came from God to give Mary wonderful news.

The angel greeted her and said, "You are blessed by the Lord!"

175

Mary was afraid. But the angel comforted her, saying, "Fear not, for you are special to God. You will have a baby boy who you will name Jesus. He will be called the Son of the Highest."

Mary said, "How can that be since I am not yet married?"

"With God nothing is impossible," the angel told her.

And Mary said, "I am the servant of the Lord."

At that time, everyone in the Holy Land had to be counted and put on a list. Mary was going to marry Joseph whose family came from Bethlehem. So they had to travel to Bethlehem to be counted, even though Mary was close to having her baby.

178

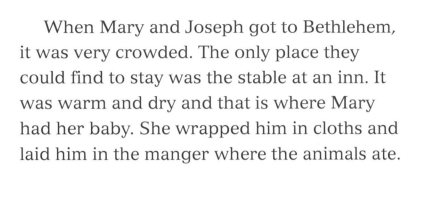

When Mary and Joseph got to Bethlehem, it was very crowded. The only place they could find to stay was the stable at an inn. It was warm and dry and that is where Mary had her baby. She wrapped him in cloths and laid him in the manger where the animals ate.

Nearby, shepherds were watching over their flocks. An angel came to them in a bright light, and they were afraid.

"Don't be afraid," said the angel. "I bring good news for everyone. Today, Christ the Lord is born. You will find the baby lying in a manger."

Suddenly, other angels joined him saying, "Glory to God! Peace on earth!"

The shepherds hurried to Bethlehem and saw Mary, Joseph, with the baby Jesus lying in a manger. Then they told everyone they met what they had seen.

The Three Wise Men: Matthew 2

After Jesus was born, three wise men came from the east to the holy city of Jerusalem.

They asked, "Where is the child who is born a king? We have seen his star and followed it to worship him."

King Herod, who ruled the land, heard about this. He was worried. Who was this child who people called a king? He told the wise men to find the child and tell him where he was.

The wise men followed the star that went before them. It led them to the house where Mary, Joseph, and Jesus were staying.

The wise men bowed down and worshipped Jesus. They gave him gold and other precious gifts.

God told them in a dream not to go back to King Herod. So they left and traveled back home another way.

An angel came to Joseph in a dream and told him King Herod was angry with them. He was to take Mary and Jesus to safety in Egypt. So, Joseph, Mary, and Jesus traveled to Egypt and lived there until Herod was dead. Then they went back to the town of Nazareth in the Holy Land.

195

Jesus the Teacher: Matthew 4

When Jesus grew up, he began to teach people about God. As he walked along the seashore one day, he saw some fishermen.

"Follow me," Jesus called to them. "I will make you fish for people."

They left their nets and followed him.

Jesus chose more people to be his helpers.
There were twelve special men, called his disciples.

Jesus

Peter

Andrew

John

James
Son of
Zebedee

Bartholom

He taught them about God, and they told others about everything they learned from Jesus.

Thaddaeus

Thomas

James
Son of
Alphaeus

Simon

Judas

Philip

Matthew

Jesus went up on a mountain to teach great crowds of people.

He said, "Be kind to everyone, even people who hurt you. If someone smacks you on one cheek, turn the other cheek, too.

Love your neighbors. But love your enemies, as well."

"Don't worry about what you eat, or drink, or wear," Jesus said. "God will take care of you. Look at the flowers—they do not work. But not even the robes of King Solomon were as bright and beautiful as they."

202

Jesus told people to pray simply.
The prayer he taught them
is called The Lord's Prayer.

Our father who is in heaven,
hallowed be your name,
your kingdom come,
your will be done
on earth as it is in heaven.
Give us this day our daily bread.
Forgive us our debts,
as we forgive our debtors.
And lead us not into temptation,
but deliver us from evil.

Jesus on the Sea: Matthew 14

One day, Jesus and his disciples needed to cross the sea. Jesus sent them on ahead in a boat. But he stayed behind to pray. Storm clouds filled the sky. Jesus saw that the disciples were in trouble in their boat.

The wind and waves tossed the boat around. Then the disciples saw someone walking on the water toward them. They thought it was a ghost. But it was Jesus. He called to them not to be afraid.

One of the men, a man named Peter, jumped out of the boat to walk on the water toward Jesus. But soon he sank right in. Jesus pulled him out and they got into the boat. They all said, "Truly you are the son of God!"

The Good Neighbor: Luke 10

Once, a clever man asked Jesus, "I know I should love my neighbor. But who exactly is my neighbor?"

So Jesus told him a story:

"A man was walking along a lonely road. Some robbers beat him and stole everything he had. He was badly hurt."

"People came along on the road, but no one stopped to help the hurt man. They all were too busy."

"Then a man called a Samaritan came by.
Samaritans were not liked by most people.
But he helped the hurt man."

"The Samaritan bandaged the man's wounds. He put him on his donkey and took him to an inn. He paid for the man to stay there until he got better."

When the story was over Jesus asked, "Who was the neighbor to the hurt man?"

The clever man said, "The one who took care of him."

Jesus said, "Go and do as he did."

The Lost Son: Luke 15

Jesus told another story:

"There was a man who had two sons. One son asked him for half of the family farm and fortune. His father gave it to him.

Before long, this son packed up his things and went away.

He spent all of that money on eating and drinking and having fun. Soon, his money was gone."

"The son was so poor he had to work feeding pigs. But he did not have enough food for himself. So, he ate the pigs' food."

"After a while, the young man thought he should go back to his father and ask for help. He traveled back to his father's farm."

"When his father saw him coming down the road, he ran to hug and kiss his son.

Then his father gave a big feast to welcome his lost son home."

Jesus told this story to show how God is like this father. Even when God's children are lost, he welcomes them back with love.

Jesus in the Holy City: Matthew 20

One day, Jesus and his disciples traveled all the way to the holy city of Jerusalem. Jesus rode into the big city on a donkey. The people of Jerusalem greeted him with joy. They laid palm branches on the road before him in welcome. They shouted, "Hosanna!" which means, "Save us!" The people called him the Son of David. That meant they believed he was the new king of Israel.

The leaders of the city grew worried. They did not like it when the people called Jesus a king. There already was a ruler of the land. They thought Jesus was causing a lot of trouble. That made them angry. These leaders did not understand that the kingdom of Jesus was really the kingdom of heaven.

It was the feast of Passover while Jesus was in Jerusalem. That is the holiday when Jewish people remember when Moses led God's people out of Egypt.

Jesus and his followers had a Passover supper in Jerusalem, like everyone else.

During the supper, Jesus broke a loaf of bread in two.

He poured out wine.

"This bread and wine is like my body and my blood,"
he said. "Eating and drinking these things will remind
you of me."

Jesus told them that he would soon be leaving them.

The Last Days of Jesus: Mark 14

Judas was one of Jesus' disciples. But he was angry with Jesus. He decided to tell the leaders of the city about Jesus. Judas wanted them to put Jesus in prison.

One night, Jesus went to a garden to pray.
His disciples were with him but they fell asleep.

Judas knew Jesus was there too. He led soldiers to the garden to take Jesus prisoner. The disciples were all afraid and ran away.

The leaders of Jerusalem decided to hand Jesus over to their ruler. He was a Roman named Pilate. Pilate did not like being bothered about Jesus. He decided to show everyone that Jesus was not a king. After asking Jesus many questions, Pilate ordered Jesus to be put to death by hanging on a wooden cross.

The day Jesus died was a terrible day. The skies grew dark and a great wind arose. Many people were afraid. Some people prayed, other people ran away to hide.

He is Risen! Matthew 28

After Jesus died, some of his friends carried his body away and laid it in a tomb.

The tomb was closed with a great
stone. Roman soldiers guarded the tomb.

Three days after Jesus died, the earth shook. An angel came and rolled the stone away from the entrance, then sat on the stone. When the soldiers saw the angel, they fell down in fear and ran.

Some of the women who followed Jesus came, weeping, to the tomb. They saw that the stone was rolled away and that Jesus was gone.

"Do not be afraid," the angel told the women. "Jesus is not here. He is risen! He is alive, again!"

Jesus' friends locked themselves in a room after Jesus died. They were afraid they would be taken prisoner by the Romans too. But, then, Jesus came to them. The disciples were amazed Jesus was alive and fell down and worshipped him.

"Peace be with you," Jesus said. Jesus then told them to go and spread the good news about what had happened.

Finally, forty days later, Jesus rose up to heaven to be with God, his father.

The followers of Jesus went out into the world and told everyone about Jesus and his wonderful story.

Saul Becomes Paul: Acts 9

There was a man named Saul who was very
angry with the followers of Jesus. He wanted to
put them all in prison. Saul found out where some
of Jesus' followers were meeting. So he set out to
take them prisoner.

But as Saul traveled, a light from heaven flashed around him. He fell to the ground.

He heard a voice that said, "Saul, Saul, why are you hurting me?"

"Who are you, Lord?" asked Saul.

"I am Jesus and you are hurting me!" said the voice.

When Saul got up, he could not see. He was taken to a follower of Jesus who took care of him. After a time Saul's sight came back. By then, he had learned a lot about Jesus and believed in Jesus. He changed his name to "Paul" to show how much he had changed.

Paul began to travel around the world preaching about Jesus. He started many churches where more and more people began to learn about Jesus and his Father's love.

Papa shut the Bible. Honey was fast asleep and Brother's and Sister's eyes were closing.

"Good night," said Papa, tucking Brother and Sister in. "God bless you!"

"'Night, Papa," murmured Brother and Sister, sleepily. "Bless you!"

Papa picked up Honey to carry her to bed.

"Bible stories were a good choice," he said to himself.

And he tip-toed softly out of the room.